AWESOME DOGS

Rottweilers

by Mari Schuh

BLASTOFF!
2
READERS

BELLWETHER MEDIA • MINNEAPOLIS, MN

Note to Librarians, Teachers, and Parents:

Blastoff! Readers are carefully developed by literacy experts and combine standards-based content with developmentally appropriate text.

Level 1 provides the most support through repetition of high-frequency words, light text, predictable sentence patterns, and strong visual support.

Level 2 offers early readers a bit more challenge through varied simple sentences, increased text load, and less repetition of high-frequency words.

Level 3 advances early-fluent readers toward fluency through increased text and concept load, less reliance on visuals, longer sentences, and more literary language.

Level 4 builds reading stamina by providing more text per page, increased use of punctuation, greater variation in sentence patterns, and increasingly challenging vocabulary.

Level 5 encourages children to move from "learning to read" to "reading to learn" by providing even more text, varied writing styles, and less familiar topics.

Whichever book is right for your reader, Blastoff! Readers are the perfect books to build confidence and encourage a love of reading that will last a lifetime!

This edition first published in 2016 by Bellwether Media, Inc.

No part of this publication may be reproduced in whole or in part without written permission of the publisher. For information regarding permission, write to Bellwether Media, Inc., Attention: Permissions Department, 5357 Penn Avenue South, Minneapolis, MN 55419.

Library of Congress Cataloging-in-Publication Data
Names: Schuh, Mari C., 1975- author.
Title: Rottweilers / by Mari Schuh.
Other titles: Blastoff! Readers. 2, Awesome Dogs.
Description: Minneapolis, MN : Bellwether Media, Inc., [2016] | Series: Blastoff! Readers. Awesome Dogs | Audience: Ages 5-8. | Audience: K to grade 3. | Includes bibliographical references and index.
Identifiers: LCCN 2015036443 | ISBN 9781626173071 (hardcover : alk. paper)
Subjects: LCSH: Rottweiler dog–Juvenile literature. | Dog breeds–Juvenile literature.
Classification: LCC SF429.R7 S38 2016 | DDC 636.73–dc23
LC record available at http://lccn.loc.gov/2015036443

Table of Contents

What Are Rottweilers?

Rottweilers are a big dog **breed**. They are strong and active.

The dogs are also
called Rotties.

Rotties have powerful bodies. Their chests are **broad**.

They usually weigh between 80 and 135 pounds (36 and 61 kilograms).

Rottweilers have short, black **coats**. Their hair is straight and **coarse**.

Markings on their coats are tan, rust, or reddish brown.

History of Rottweilers

Rottweilers are named after the German town of Rottweil. The breed **officially** started there in the early 1900s.

Germany

N W E S

But the breed's beginnings go
back 2,000 years earlier!

Back then, Roman **troops** kept dogs to move sheep and cattle. They needed the herds for food.

Eventually, the dogs came to Germany with the soldiers. There, they **bred** with other herding dogs.

The new breed was known
for being tough and fearless.
They worked as military dogs
and police dogs.

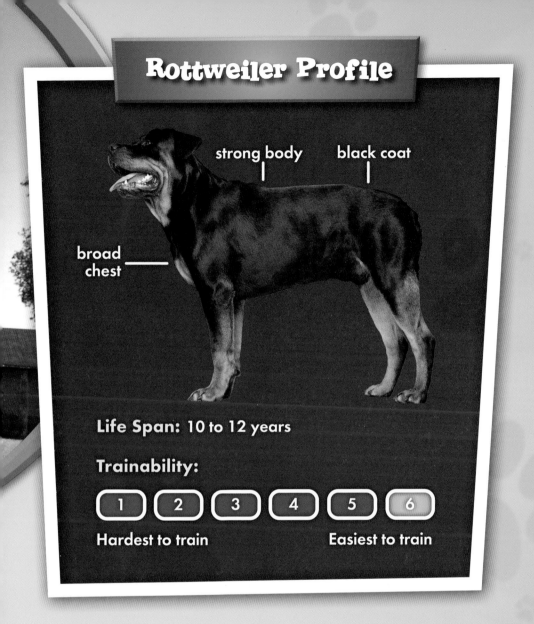

Rottweiler Profile

strong body

black coat

broad chest

Life Span: 10 to 12 years

Trainability:

| 1 | 2 | 3 | 4 | 5 | 6 |

Hardest to train   Easiest to train

Today, Rottweilers are in the **Working Group** of the **American Kennel Club**.

Smart and Loyal

Rottweilers are smart dogs. But they need training.

Owners should start training
Rotties when they are puppies.

Rottweilers want to **protect** their owners from strangers.

They also want to please their owners. They are very **loyal** dogs.

Rottweilers can be great family pets. They are loving and playful.

Some even act silly!

Glossary

American Kennel Club—an organization that keeps track of dog breeds in the United States

bred—produced offspring

breed—a type of dog

broad—wide

coarse—rough

coats—the hair or fur covering some animals

loyal—having constant support for someone

officially—became publicly known

protect—to keep safe

troops—groups of soldiers

Working Group—a group of dog breeds that have a history of performing jobs for people

To Learn More

AT THE LIBRARY
Graubart, Norman D. *My Dog*. New York, N.Y.:
PowerKids Press, 2014.

Johnson, Jinny. *Rottweiler*. Mankato, Minn.: Smart
Apple Media, 2015.

Shores, Erika L. *All About Rottweilers*. North
Mankato, Minn.: Capstone Press, 2013.

ON THE WEB
Learning more about Rottweilers
is as easy as 1, 2, 3.

1. Go to www.factsurfer.com.

2. Enter "Rottweilers" into the search box.

3. Click the "Surf" button and you will see a
   list of related web sites.

With factsurfer.com, finding more
information is just a click away.

Index